TIMELESS

Design

TIMELESS
Design

BO NILES

Foreword by Wendy Moonan

Contributing Editor, Architecture
CONDÉ NAST
House&Garden

PBC INTERNATIONAL, INC.

Distributor to the book trade in the United States and Canada
Rizzoli International Publications
through St. Martin's Press
175 Fifth Avenue
New York, NY 10010

Distributor to the art trade in the United States and Canada
PBC International, Inc.
One School Street
Glen Cove, NY 11542

Distributor throughout the rest of the world
Hearst Books International
1350 Avenue of the Americas
New York, NY 10019

Library of Congress Cataloging-in-Publication Data

Niles, Bo.
Timeless design / by Bo Niles
    p.   cm.
  Includes index.
  ISBN 0-86636-543-5 (hc : alk. paper). — ISBN 0-86636-544-3 (pb :alk. paper)
  1. Design—History—20th century. 2. Classicism—Influence. I. Title.
NK1390.N52 1997   96-49986
745.2'09'04—dc21   CIP

CAVEAT– Information in this text is believed accurate, and will pose no
problem for the student or casual reader. However, the author was often
constrained by information contained in signed release forms, information
that could have been in error or not included at all. Any misinformation
(or lack of information) is the result of failure in these attestations. The
author has done whatever is possible to insure accuracy.

Designed by Garrett Schuh

Color separation by Fine Arts Repro House Co., Ltd., H.K.
Printed in Hong Kong by South China Printing Co. (1988) Ltd.

10 9 8 7 6 5 4 3 2 1

Printed in Hong Kong

*To Dylan
and the Design Writers Group
colleagues
and dear friends*

CONTENTS

FOREWORD

hat is "timeless" design? Is it eternal? Hardly. Does it have a beginning or end? Of course it does. Architecture and interior design are linked to their era by style, custom, materials and function. The Viennese Secessionists perhaps said it best a century ago when, rejecting the ponderous neoclassicism of the Austro-Hungarian Empire, they promoted the Wiener Werkstätte style with the rallying cry, "To each age its art."

Nonetheless, we all know that some rooms, from the mirrored halls of the Hotel Lambert in Paris to the late Billy Baldwin's New York City apartment, wear well over time. These pleasing environments, often conforming to proportions of the Golden Mean, and endowed with appropriate but distinctive furniture, and eclectic art collections, share one trait: true personality. In the projects that New York writer Bo Niles presents on the following pages, splendid residences that range from Los Angeles to Rome, designers are not trying to do what's never been done before. They insist on proper scale, spaces that flow, layouts that function, furniture that puts us at ease and materials we won't tire of. They know how to capture light and make it magical. Even when it's clear that teams of specialists have been required and attention to detail has been more rigorous than usual, these spaces do not seem contrived. They are profoundly appealing, memorable, and stylish—without being merely trendy or fashionable. They, too, have personality. The talents who created these interiors display vision, daring, ingenuity and wit. Their styles vary, but they are all disciplined thinkers who know how to edit objects in such a way that the spaces endure. Now, *that's* timeless.

Wendy Moonan
Contributing Editor, Architecture
Condé Nast House & Garden

INTRODUCTION

The threshold of any decade is a time for taking stock of where we have been, reassessing what we know—or think we know—and speculating upon where we are headed. As a millennium approaches, this exercise intensifies, and every principle we hold dear, it seems, is called into question.

During the twentieth century, advances in technology shaped and reshaped each decade with increasing velocity. Hurtled into the so-called space age, we have been forced to alter our expectations for the future, causing us to raise many questions about where we live, how we live, and what we live with. At the heart of this questioning is our very definition of "home."

Design, of course, is integral to the notion of home. The dictionary defines design as both "particular" and "purposeful": An underlying scheme informs an arrangement of elements, to the service of a predisposed aesthetic. Design may be open to interpretation, but it is founded upon established tenets and harmonies.

Design is an ongoing process, yet it also reflects a specific point in the evolution of a body of work; a particular design, in other words, reflects what the designer or architect is thinking about at that moment. And so, even if they are expected to stand the test of time, designs of our generation—and homes of the 1990s—will, of necessity, impart an aura or flavor of this current decade, the period in which they were created.

If there is a point to be made in the final analysis of what underlies today's philosophy of timeless design as expressed by the projects that follow, it is that a living space must reveal an essential integrity and harmony both within and without. A house or apartment must be appropriate to its setting and to the lifestyle of its occupants. It cannot be a mere ego trip for an architect or interior designer.

To be livable, manageable, and comfortable, spaces work best when they are restrained in demeanor and pared down in decoration. Materials in every case should be—and are, in every instance on the pages that follow—of the finest quality possible; craftsmanship should be—and is—impeccably executed; movement throughout the space should be—and is—traced in a logical flow. An appreciation and concern for the environment also prevails. In these places, precious little is wasted; one feels the essence of the space and the absolute rightness of the selection of what enhances and fills that space.

Once the architectural surround is established, and the furnishings are arranged in an appropriate manner, then humor and idiosyncrasy can—and often do—emerge in the details, such as the selection and placement of artworks, artifacts, and accessories. For without humor—be it dry or wry, or even of a slapstick quality—life ebbs from a home, and when that happens, that home freezes, in its attitude—and in time.

As architect Jeff Parsons, of Parsons + Fernandez-Casteleiro concludes: "'Timeless' infers opportunities that are not immediate, while 'design' is an activity that explores the immediacy of space perceptions. Combined, they result in a way of thinking in a new dimension, one that can ignore conventional references."

When those results are comfortable to live with, then "timeless design" is no longer an oxymoron; it is a celebration of day-to-day and decade-to-decade living—and of everything home should be.

ARCHITECTURAL

In timeless dwellings, structural elements tend to be distilled to their essence, disclosing a reverence for space and light. The skeletal envelope might, upon occasion, seem stark, but is often gentled with details such as a molding, a shoji-inspired partition, a color-washed surface. Against such a background, furnishings may comfortably assume a stylishness tethered to no particular era.

ELBASANI AND LOGAN
A Courtyard Shelter

If a site is dramatic, it makes sense to engage every one of its positive attributes in the design of a house while downplaying any negatives. When planning a residence for themselves and their three children in Berkeley, California, Donn Logan, FAIA of ELS and Marcy Li Wong, AIA harnessed the plusses: volcanic boulders, mature shrubs and trees, abundant light, and a view of San Francisco Bay. To protect themselves from too much sun and wind, though, they decided to construct the house as a series of wings around a courtyard. The progression of spaces culminates in a grand, tri-level studio they call the Great Room. The master bedroom and the children's rooms occupy opposite ends of the floor plan, but, as a crow flies, they stand conveniently catercorner to each other across the court. Interiors emphasize spaciousness with simple furnishings, including some revered classics, such as a bentwood rocker and Alvar Aalto stools.

above *Integrating house and site informed the selection of materials, including concrete masonry block and tongue-in-groove cedar siding.*

opposite *The uppermost level of the Great Room is devoted to dining as it adjoins the kitchen. Grooves crisscrossing the concrete floors echo window grids.*

photography by
David Wakely

right *Ceilings in the tri-level Great Room telescope from 10 feet to 14 feet to 18 feet; a series of beam-bracketed window bays along both side walls follows the progression, much like a majestic, stately march.*

below *The middle level of the Great Room is dedicated to music, and to a library. Railings painted green and tipped with red set up a lively syncopation against white-and-taupe walls. The living room level accommodates two work stations as well as the piano.*

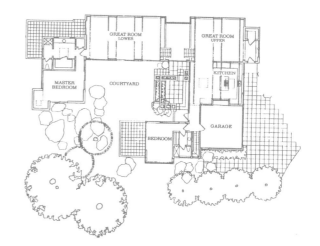

left *Pale beech cabinetry warms the kitchen; countertops are granite burnished to a fine sheen. The slatted ceiling diffuses light from a pair of skylights. Molded plywood chairs surround an antique pine table.*

above *The courtyard is treated like an outdoor room, with a raised patio for seating and a lawn-carpeted enclosure for sunning. Slatted blinds, which match the trellis, swing out to shade the interiors.*

ANGELO TARTAGLIA
Honoring the Context

Throughout history, a number of buildings so persuasively synthesize aspects of their cultural environment and period that they become icons of their age. Like the Parthenon or the villas of Palladio, for example, they are timeless in their appeal. Angelo Tartaglia sought to encapsulate the essence of the current decade in the residence he renovated for the owner of a major Italian olive oil company. He also wanted the house to stand out from its "chaos" of a neighborhood, where the surrounding buildings present a cacophony of styles. The powerful external image he came up with is blunt and straightforward: a simple "volume" accented by minimally embellished apertures. Inside, high-tech references, such as an overarching roof/ceiling formed of corrugated steel, perpetuates the architect's notion that placing this home within a contemporary context will allow it to be as exciting to look at and live in in the future as it is today.

above *The house presents an uncluttered, austere facade. Unfinished terracing and arched front door mimic the arc of the vaulted roof.*

opposite *The top floor belongs to the owners' son. The ceiling was painted white to avoid rust; the cylinder contains the bath.*

photography by *Edoardo d'Antona*

Campobasso, Italy   3,168 Square Feet • 294 Square Meters

left *Countertops of Corian, and cabinets of M.D.F. lacquer were designed to be as sleek and maintenance-free as possible. Double doors lead back into the laundry and service areas.*

opposite *Tartaglia designed the island, capping it with oak for a warm look. The track lighting bar accommodates both fluorescent and halogen systems, the latter on transformers.*

above *Tartaglia wanted to create an otherworldly atmosphere in the loft, so he complemented the vaulted ceiling with portholes. Red leather chairs are by Roberto Felicetti; the desk, by the architect himself. Flooring is of a wood called* afromosia.

right *It goes without saying that a family in the olive oil business would desire a large kitchen, and Tartaglia acceded to their wishes. The opaque, gridded windows comply with an Italian law that prohibits peering into a neighbor's property.*

opposite *The so-called "canopy"*
bedroom boasts a voluptuous
late-18th-century chest in the
ornate Italian barocco style; it is
just one of a collection of pieces
the family inherited and
brought into the house once
renovations were complete. The
owner's mother-in-law
crocheted the cover on the bed.

above *Marble is so plentiful in*
Italy, it was used on walls, floors
and countertops in all of the
bathrooms; for three of these,
Tartaglia specified calacatta
marble from Tuscany.

right *The daughter's bathroom*
appearance was softened by
the introduction of salmon-hued
curtains into the design scheme.

THAD HAYES
The Acid Test

Striking the right balance between wit and wisdom, in design and in life, is no easy task; one false move tilts the scale to facetiousness or pedantry. When an art dealer in Manhattan retained designer Thad Hayes to renovate her residence, she sought to reconcile an uptown/downtown dialectic—sophistication with street-smarts. Hayes suavely achieved her aim by capitalizing on the friction set up by virile, assertive artworks and voluptuous, highly tactile furnishings which he meticulously arranged within a classically proportioned shell. A strong focal point, such as the zebra wood mantelpiece in the living room, anchors each room. Soft light suffuses the spaces from a mix of sources: windows tempered with sheers, sconces, a chandelier, and sculptural table and floor lamps. Hayes combined 1940s and '50s furnishings from France and Italy with pieces of his own design. Thus, the entire assembly is a work of art in its own right.

above *A pair of 1950s Italian armchairs in blue satin face Hayes's sofa across a coffee table of the same period designed by Gilbert Poillerat.*

photography by *Michael Mundy*

above *The living room plays off subtle alterations in surface and plane that are eloquently expressed by the interrelationship between wall, chimneypiece, mirror, artworks—and untrimmed openings to the hall.*

For a room to endure, it must incorporate daily experiences into the design process.

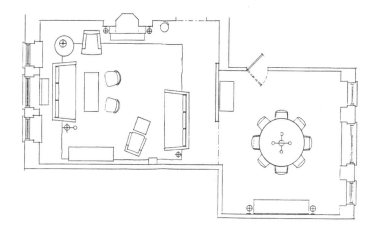

left *A David Salle diptych squares off against the mantelpiece rendered by craftsman John Fisher to Thad Hayes's specifications. Its subtle striping echoes the corrugations in the leather-banded sisal area rug.*

above *In the living room, curvacious furniture is spiked with zingy color to offset paintings by prominent contemporary artists such as Francesco Clemente—and to spark conversation.*

right *The room is divided into two distinct, yet overlapping zones. An acid-green velvet sofa of Hayes's design fronts the window alongside a sexy chanteuse floor lamp topped by a stretchy shade, also by Hayes. The lipstick-red bar is lacquered to a fine sheen. Tilt-back wing chair is by Jean Royère.*

left *One end of the bedroom is dedicated to a seating area. Wall-to-wall carpeting assures quiet and softness underfoot.*

left *At the precise center of the dining room stands a pedestal table designed by Hayes in wenge wood. Pascaud chairs date from 1940; the chandelier is by Jean Royère.*

above *Furnishings and accessories in the bedroom are kept to a minimum: a blond bed by Jules Leleu flanked by a pair of tables found at the Paris puces and wall shelf by Michel Zadounisky.*

GOODMAN CHARLTON
At Home with Collections

The 1950s witnessed a huge surge in home-building. The war was over; the boys were home. As in the fairy tale, everyone wanted to live happily ever after. The optimistic new homeowner relished being in and of that moment in time. Over the years, many 1950s houses remained structurally secure, but cosmetically they suffered. Such was the case with one particular house in Los Angeles that Jeffrey Goodman and Steven Charlton of Goodman Charlton Inc. defined as a stylistic "cross between Donna Reed and Mildred Pierce." In the makeover of the house, the team peeled back the layers to reveal its "good bones," then soothed the interiors with a palette of soft greens, ochres and creams—punched with an occasional shot of a hot hue such as chartreuse. Rooms were opened up so they would flow naturally from one to the other, and on out to the garden. Within the tranquil setting, collections of photography, art, ceramics and glassware thrive.

above *Goodman Charlton designed most furnishings in the living room—and the house—for an obvious, reason: for comfort.*

opposite *The sun room also functions as a media room and library. The transition from hardwood to limestone floors appears almost seamless.*

photography by
Steven Charlton

opposite *Because the owners entertain often, the core of the house is also the dining room. Guests are invited to relax in the plush armchairs before and after the meal. The designers opened the ceiling to the roofline, painted it white, and punctuated it with skylights to amplify the sense of space. The chandelier, made from antler, is also white.*

above *A mirror leaning against the wall in the living room reflects the symbiosis of the casual and formal: luxe fabrics serving cozy seating; pictures placed on floor, ledge or wall; wood floors bleached for glamour—and slicked with polyurethane to welcome bare or stockinged feet.*

left *Fireplaces in the living room and dining room—and their wood box—are contrived as works of art that perfectly complement the actual works of art resting on or near them. Doors are trimmed to frame views to adjacent rooms and the garden in much the same way.*

opposite *With its walls of windows, the sunroom creates a natural transition from the living/dining area to the garden behind the house.*

above *The cool wicker seating and tile-topped table perfectly complement the jungle-like plantings, and impart a "colonial/raj" aura to the outdoor setting.*

ARTHUR de MATTOS CASAS
A Neutral Envelope

Upon occasion, the desires of a client may be subsumed to the ego of the designer, which typically handicaps the comfort of the client as well as the overall design. For Arthur de Mattos Casas, good design must be humane: "Timeless design," he writes, "outlives fashion and gives priority to man and his needs"—in this case to those of a young businessman who travels often. Moving into a contemporary, multilevel house that had initially been constructed as a family dwelling, the client requested that the architect tailor it to his casual, practical lifestyle. De Mattos Casas complied by distilling both design and client requests to basics. What he and his staff created, in essence, is a neutral, open-plan envelope in which spare groupings of clean-lined, contemporary furnishings defer to an evolving collection of books, paintings and *objets d'art* culled from around the world. Here, everything has a place and there is a place for everything: an impeccable example of a cliché turned into an adage of superlative design.

above *In the dining area, dowel-studded, steel-armed chairs designed in the de Mattos Casas studio surround a classic Saarinen table from the 1950s.*

photography by
Tuca Reinés/Reinés Studio

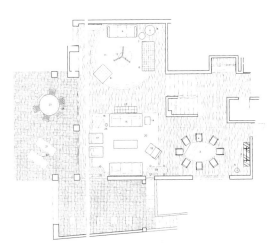

below *The living area is positioned at the core of the house and thus readily accesses all public spaces.*

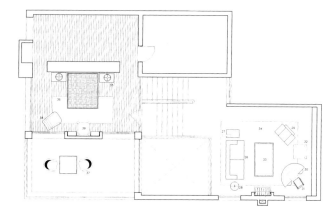

De Mattos Casas designed the master bedroom all of a piece. The bed and storage cabinet comprise one monolithic unit which floats upon a near-bare wood floor. Lighting throughout the house is unobtrusive and suited to the task.

right *The upper story of the house is shared by a master suite and a private sitting area (also a balcony overlook) where a collection of wooden boxes inscribed with Japanese calligraphy is complemented by a twisting Akari lamp by Isamu Noguchi.*

EMANUELA FRATTINI MAGNUSSON
The Best of Both Worlds

If it weren't for historic preservationists, too many noteworthy buildings in our cities would be razed; occasionally, though, missionary zeal can override the actual merits of a structure. Luckily, in the case of a turn-of-the-century brownstone in a landmarked district in Manhattan that architect Emanuela Frattini Magnusson was invited to modernize for a Scandinavian client, only the facade was deemed "untouchable." No laws governed the interiors or rear of the structure. Gutted to its shell, the five-story building was re-composed into a bright and airy residence. A Scandinavian sensibility is felt throughout: in the use of pale maple wood and a neutral color scheme to capitalize on light, and in the spare arrangement of furnishings calculated to comfort. To augment the sense of harmony throughout the building, the architect designed a "ribbon" of a stair to connect all five floors; the stair, visible from virtually every room, serves as the primary architectural element and focus of the house.

above *The town house blends in with its near neighbors.*

opposite *Living-room bookcases rise past the balcony to the 23-foot ceiling.* Pate de verre *glass fastened with steel bolts frames the fireplace. Seating is wrapped in white cotton; sheer linen panels screen the windows. Limb-like sculpture is from Nigeria.*

photography by
Jürgen Frank

opposite *The dining room can be closed off by a bi-fold door made of corrugated plywood. The large slate on the wall is often used as an ad hoc blackboard. Cabinets run underneath. A rare set of Arne Jacobsen armchairs on casters pull around the table. The overhead fixture is Spanish.*

below *Cabinetry in the kitchen is offset by a green laminate back-splash and countertops molded of a concrete-resin mixture dyed dark grey. The table, straddling a cabinet that serves as an island, is topped by the same concrete. Stools are by Aalto; "Titania" light fixture is from Luceplan.*

left *The Scandinavian tradition of wrapping a handrail in leather is replicated on the town house stair. The opposing banister was fabricated of steel.*

above *The "ribbon" stair can be viewed as a sculptural entity traveling up through the stairwell to every floor.*

right *In one of the front bedrooms, the bed, custom-crafted by Pierluigi Ghianda in Milan, is dressed in natural linen. Slim radiators tuck tidily under the windows. The sculpture—Vine— is by Alexander Calder.*

left *Great attention was paid to cabinetry and fittings in the bedrooms, and throughout the house, to maintain a pure, consistent appearance. All wood is maple; all pulls, from Knoll International.*

below *A close-up of one of the beds reveals the owner's affinity for simple effects. Rugs, from Elizabeth Eakins, were woven especially for the house.*

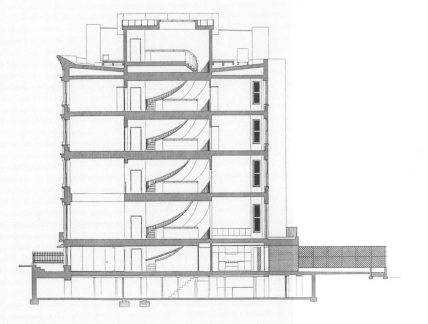

ORLANDO DIAZ-AZCUY
A Minimalist Approach

To stand the test of time, design must neither ignore historic precedent nor shun implications of what the future holds. Designer Orlando Diaz-Azcuy sought to balance the abstract best of old and new when he renovated a Victorian house in San Francisco fifteen years ago. Although generally adverse to ornament, he was charmed by the "spirit" and gracious proportions of the mid-19th-century rooms, so when he gutted the interiors, he heeded the original layout and replicated period baseboards and window trim. Cornices and other overbearing architectural elements he felt would stifle his modernist design were eliminated, and all surfaces smoothed to prepare them for a luxurious cloak of high-gloss paint. Diaz-Azcuy honored the Victorian penchant for differentiating rooms in a way that is at once adroit and astonishing: openings between the public spaces soar to the 11½-foot-high ceilings while access to the private zones, by contrast, occurs via narrow arches and standard doorways.

above *A sculptural bookcase separates the library from the dining room. Recessed spots cast pools of light upon the bare, bleached oak-strip floors.*

photography by
Jaime Ardiles-Arce

previous *In a corner of the living room, a 17th-century Venetian settee covered in yellow silk taffeta keeps company with a Mies van der Rohe armchair clad in burgundy mohair; a Saarinen table stands between them.*

above *The living room chimneypiece juts out from a mirrored wall, which reflects a pair of 40-inch-high Italian vases from the early 19th century.*

right *The flow through the apartment is enhanced by subtle gradations of a single hue, green, spanning five whisper-soft tints, from celadon to jade.*

DI CICCO VINCI • AHN ARCHITECTS
A Study in Serenity

Bringing old and new ideas into accord is an explicit aim of designers intent upon achieving an atmosphere of timelessness. In some cases, the "old" is a given: a structure that requires updating may boast some appealing elements that beg to be respected and retained. James Ahn and Carol Di Cicco Vinci were presented with just such a scenario when they were asked to rejuvenate an aging prewar apartment on Manhattan's Fifth Avenue. The building allowed no relocation of plumbing or gas lines, but otherwise the layout could be redesigned to accommodate the owners' desire for a well-defined yet tranquil environment. Both owners and architects wanted to make subtle reference to a few existing architectural details. They also wanted to re-introduce a traditional ploy that was curiously lacking—a foyer—to set off public rooms and separate them from private zones. New millwork, by contrast, is clean-lined and virtually unadorned, and furnishings minimized to emphasize space and light.

above *The new foyer mediates between the living room (at the far end of the photograph) and the dining room. Bare maple floors unite all spaces.*

Photography by
Michael Moran

right *To encourage a sense of translucency, doorways and openings between foyer, hall, and public spaces were widened and pulled up to ceiling height; doors were fitted with panels of clear and crackled glass. A mosaic "rug" was recessed into the floor and a ceiling fixture custom-made for the space.*

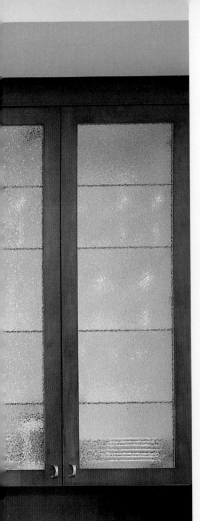

left *As a contemporary twist, a drop of violet was added to the stain used on all millwork. Doors between dining room cabinets open to a guest room furnished with a slinky chaise.*

above *Bathrooms were completely refurbished. Tilework plays out in compatible patterns. Freestanding lavs were custom designed.*

above right *Although the kitchen is compact, it fulfills the requirements of its owner, a professional chef. Cracked-tile mosaicwork recurs as a leitmotif.*

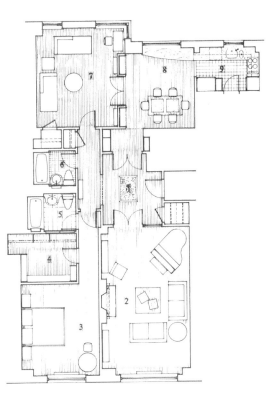

OLSON SUNDBERG
Celebrating Natural Materials

When dwellingplaces are created to reflect regional as well as timeless ideologies, architectural references to place can be covert or subtle. A condominium complex designed by the Seattle firm Olson Sundberg Architects makes a frankly contemporary outward statement, but also evokes the design heritage specific to the Northwest, an area renowned for its ecofriendly attitude and generous use of natural materials, expecially wood. The apartment featured here hewed to these principles with particular empathy. One of its owners suffers from Multiple Chemical Sensitivity and cannot tolerate toxins or chemicals. This proclivity coupled with a Japanese aesthetic inspired a healthy interior environment that celebrates natural materials in their natural state—including woods and fibers that have been untreated in any way. For the most part, the color palette in the apartment relies upon warm woodsy tones, except for accents of yellow, which the owners feel to be a fresh, uplifting hue.

above *The condominium's angular, zigzagged exterior capitalizes on views and light through its extensive use of glass—and decks.*

photography by
Michael Jensen

Kirkland, Washington   3,016 Square Feet • 280 Square Meters

right *The dual home office, with its shared U-shaped desktop and banks of wall cabinets, tucks into a small room overlooking a garden.*

below *All interior spaces in the ground floor apartment are connected by a "spine of light." Wood utilized throughout is unstained maple. The robe is Japanese.*

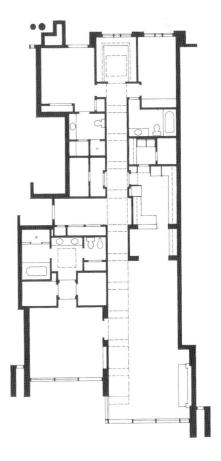

FORD, POWELL & CARSON
Wedded to Nature

Some houses deliberately stand out from their sites; others, by contrast, are discreetly integrated into their natural surround. To feel timeless, the latter, by extension, usually respect the vernacular of the region—be it Tuscany or Texas. For a couple who desired a weekend retreat for their extended family, San Antonio-based Chris Carson, FAIA and interior designer John Gutzler, ASID, of the firm Ford, Powell & Carson, wanted to celebrate a spectacular site in the Texas Hill Country that contemplates a sinuous bend in the Guadalupe River fringed by ancient cypress trees. To take advantage of the views across the lawn to the river, the firm relied on one of architecture's classic forms, a steep-pitched A, which nimbly embraces wide expanses of glass. Most materials within the house are indigenous to the area: bleached mesquite, for example, covers the floors; stone, quarried nearby, was installed with big grout joints, a feature typical to houses in this part of the country.

above *The main seating group in the fir-sheathed living room is supplemented by a game table surrounded by chairs of woven leather.*

opposite *For comfort, the living room sofas are upholstered in chenille. A salvaged cypress stump functions as an end table.*

photography by *Blaine Hickey, Ogden Robertson/Hickey-Robertson*

opposite *A huge pine lodgepole four-poster commissioned for the master bedroom is warmed by an antique "Log Cabin" quilt. Upholstery here, as in the living room, is chenille; the carpeting was custom designed and woven from 100 percent wool. The fireplace surround is green slate.*

above *A gallery connects the main house to its bedroom wing. Track lighting along the ceiling targets the antique table and benches made to match and a screen fabricated from willow sticks. Hickory chairs feature woven leather stripping and down-filled seat cushions.*

DENNIS JENKINS AND BERNARD ZYSCOVICH
In a Zen-like Mood

To effect the metamorphosis of a dated dwellingplace into a timeless habitat, designers often turn to the architecture and aesthetic of Japan for inspiration. Such was the case with the residence pictured here, a 1950s ranch house in southern Florida. The owners travel extensively in the Far East and appreciate the reverence for natural materials and emphasis on simplicity they encountered in Japan. In the first phase of an ongoing renovation of their house, the team of Dennis Jenkins, interior designer, and Bernard Zyscovich, architect, concurred with their bias; a new master suite is the result. In Japan, space is often at a premium; here, by contrast, a generous room size prevails. The sense of tranquility and repose that pervades the master suite is counterbalanced by spicy doses of vivid color reminiscent of an emperor's robe, manifest in the sumptuous bedclothes and in the large tripartite painting that hangs over the bed.

above *A skylit corridor links the master bedroom, dressing area and bath. Mahogany floors were left unadorned.*

opposite *In the Zen-like master suite, every object is considered precious, and is positioned to be admired.*

photography by *Nancy Robinson Watson*

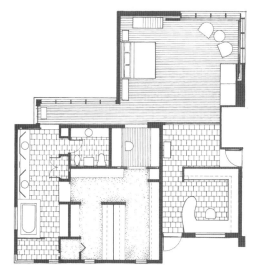

previous spread *A cantilevered beam over the bed houses recessed fixtures which bathe the painting and stepped* tansu *in light. Windsor chairs are Danish, by Hans Wegner.*

above *The open dressing area is organized with considerable finesse so clothes fit into correctly sized compartments.*

right *In the slate-floored bath, a black soaking tub stands at one end of a long low cabinet containing twin washstations.*

opposite *Visual harmonies were established by the syncopated window treatment, which layers shoji-like panels over boldly gridded windows.*

LEGORRETA ARQUITECTOS
Planned for Posterity

One way an architectural or design firm can determine if a building has the potential to endure is to solicit the opinions of a quorum of voices. Do aspects of the design seem overly contrived; do they capitulate to fashion or fad? Although architect Victor Legorreta and his colleagues repeat this exercise with every project on their drawing boards, he felt hesitant to subject his own home to the inevitable conflict between ego and consensus. After all, shouldn't an architect be able to experiment wholeheartedly with ideas and materials when there is no client but himself to please? Well, yes and no. Legorreta wanted this house to mature with his wife, Jacinta, and their children and to envelop them gracefully through every stage of their lives. Thus, simplicity won out over virtuosity, discretion triumphed over showmanship. In the Mexican tradition, this modern hacienda encircles a private patio. Spaces are flexible—perfect for a family growing up together.

above *In color and form, the entry to the house echoes the work of Luis Barragan. Legorreta considers color an emotional element that can be changed at whim.*

opposite *Doubling the ceiling height in the library adds to its atmosphere of cool surrender. The black spiral stair makes a sculptural statement, as does the marquetry table.*

photography by
Lourdes Legorreta

Rooms in a timeless house will survive any and all changes in function and furnishing.

left *The gallery looks onto the central patio. Low walls were introduced into the public interior spaces to prevent any one area from feeling at a remove from another.*

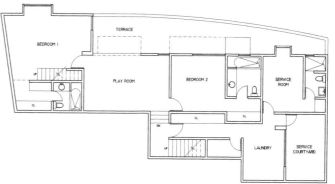

ARTHUR DE MATTOS CASAS
Straddling the Centuries

For an architect or designer, the conclusion of a millennium is a time for asking questions and reassessing the past. As the 20th century draws to a close, what facets of the arts and technologies of this last century are worth remembering? For Arthur de Mattos Casas, this is the predominant question that informs the work of his office. Quick to negate what he terms "radicalisms," he seeks to bring his affinity for contemporary forms into equilibrium with references to the past, and specifically to a historical context that is quintessentially Brazilian. A house built on a wooded plot outside the city center of São Paulo evolved into an exercise in exploring these issues. De Mattos Casas admits to weaving many artistic threads into his architectural tapestry, including the influences of Glasgow, the Bauhaus, and, naturally, Brazilian architectural themes of the 1950s and '60s. Despite these philosophical machinations, though, his intent was simple: to create a comfortable home that would last into the next century.

above *In the dining room, chairs wearing geometric "capes" of "ivory wood" surround a glass-topped table which reflects floors, and walls, of similar wood.*

photography by
Tuca Reinés

above *Motorized skylights direct breezes into the spacious living room. Except for a lipstick-hued chair, a neutral palette prevails—to set off paintings and objects, such as a whimsically striped airplane.*

Timeless design outlives fashion and gives priority to human needs.

ANGELO TARTAGLIA
A Polished Interior

A break with tradition and the past often ushers in a revitalized sensitivity toward what can and will endure. Roman architect Angelo Luigi Tartaglia fervently believes that the new technologies and materials appearing in Italy during the 1920s and '30s freed Italian architecture of prior constraints, and set a standard that continues to influence him, and others of his generation, in their contemporary work. A residence he masterminded for a leading Italian lighting designer in the Appia Antica district just outside Rome reflects his philosophy, and is marked by the Italian affinity for sparsely furnished open spaces highlighted by smooth, polished surfaces and choice works of art. To lend character to the essentially featureless spaces of this two-story home, the architect devised a handsome polychrome terrazzo floor which not only serves to unify the interlocking spaces on the ground floor, but also looks like a giant work of art—like the mosaic floors of ancient Rome.

above *The broad sweep of the terràzzo floor in the living room, and elsewhere in the house, is unbroken by rugs.*

opposite *A pair of matching white sofas and a glass coffee table, from Fiam, delineate the conversation area in the living room.*

photography by
Edoardo d'Antona

above *Tartaglia designed the cherrywood cabinet as a salute to the Deco style. The floor lamp—a fine piece in the owner's collection—is by Gianluigi Pieruzzi for Barovier & Toso. Glassware on the tabletop is Venetian.*

opposite *A potted olive tree gracefully alludes to the Italian countryside. Paintings, by Michele Crocco, were clipped to steel bars suspended from behind a dropped "cornice" to avoid punching holes in the walls.*

above *A cherrywood-and-glass vitrine separates the living room and hallway; here the owner exhibits an 18th-century Boulle clock, two Etruscan vases and an Etruscan capitello.*

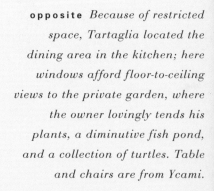

opposite *Because of restricted space, Tartaglia located the dining area in the kitchen; here windows afford floor-to-ceiling views to the private garden, where the owner lovingly tends his plants, a diminutive fish pond, and a collection of turtles. Table and chairs are from Ycami.*

above *Frosted glass panels slide into wall-pockets between rooms; thus no one area is completely cut off from another, and light can slice through. The curved wall in the kitchen backs a cabinet in the adjoining living room.*

right *The kitchen follows an unabashedly sleek and contemporary format, a collaboration of Tartaglia with the Boffi company. Cabinets are cherry; countertops, white Corian. Two integral sinks are set in the corner, near a window.*

HUGH NEWELL JACOBSEN
Variation on a Theme

When asked to draw a house, children from many cultures will sketch a generic pitch-roofed box that looks remarkably like a game piece for a Monopoly set. Invited to design a weekend retreat for a family with young children in Ontario, Hugh Newell Jacobsen, FAIA noticed this quintessential structure echoed everywhere he drove as he inspected the site and its environs. In a snow belt, the "monopoly" form proves exceptionally efficient: the gutterless pitched roof effectively sheds precipitation; the box can be as cozy or airy as desired. Jacobsen shaved the site—a cliff overhanging a lake—and carpeted it with lawn, then strung out six interlocking "pavilions" upon the turf, much like game pieces upon a board. The pavilions organize the spaces in a logical succession of public and private zones. A "street" runs through and bisects the pavilions; complementary spaces face each other across the passage. White paint and bluestone tie it all together.

above *On the exterior of the 18-foot-high pavilions, Jacobsen manipulated the perception of scale by juxtaposing large and small gridded windows.*

opposite *Symmetrically-arranged furniture floats in the center of each pavillion to give the illusion of greater space. In the living room, Jacobsen adapted the 18th-century conceit of hanging a strip of molding over the firebox instead of installing a full mantel.*

photography by
Robert C. Lautman

JAMES L. NAGLE
Exploding the Envelope

Almost every city in the world indulges a pastiche of architectural formats. Indeed, the timeless quality of a metropolis often derives from the imprint of many builders, both recognized and unknown. Buildings rise and fall, many of the fallen not missed at all. Chicago has always been judged a gutsy, vital burg, so gutting one of its standard 25-foot-wide lots to make way for a new town house caused no raised eyebrows. The couple who purchased the plot—empty-nesters moving in from the suburbs with an art collection they prize—wanted their residence to highlight the art, and be practical to maintain. Architect James L. Nagle, FAIA of the firm Nagle Hartray & Associates fractured the traditional confines of a town house. The central core—which stacks baths, closets and laundry—cants to the perimeter; a two-story triangular bay of windows pierces the facade at the same angle, as do enclosed and open balconies at the rear. Light suffuses spaces, yet privacy is maintained.

above *Although a modernist at heart, Nagle clad the new house in brick in deference to the street. The staircase leads down to a private garden behind the house.*

photography by
Hedrich Blessing

Chicago, Illinois   3,000 Square Feet   •   279 Square Meters

above *The shipshape kitchen was planned as a step-saving corridor overlooking the breakfast table. All wall-cabinet storage is tidily concealed behind spring-lock doors freed of hardware. Recessed spots evenly distribute light throughout the entire space.*

above *Three tiers of glass brick draw light into the dining area, which adjoins the living room. Chairs may pull over into the conversational group as necessary. Hardwood flooring parallels the canted core; taupe stair-tread carpet echoes the back-wall hue.*

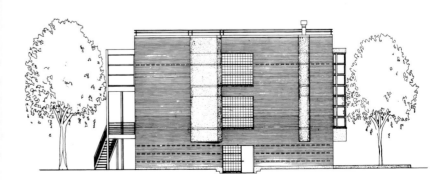

opposite *An interior balcony is suspended over the living area, which is furnished with several of Mies van der Rohe's classic Barcelona pieces. To enhance the open feeling of the double-height space, both stairway and balcony affect a taut, nautical look.*

below *The master bed and the cabinet at its foot align precisely, in a circumspect manner that gives the art room to breathe.*

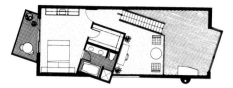

PARSONS + FERNANDEZ-CASTELEIRO
A Minimalist Aerie

By their function, certain buildings seem to transcend all temporal and spatial bounds. Many hotels fall into this category; a guest in one of them could be anywhere. An international businessman who coincidentally owns a group of hotels sought just that atmosphere of allusive comfort when he retained architects Jeff Parsons and Manuel Fernandez-Casteleiro to renovate an apartment in New York City. Their intensely cerebral exercise in refinement and restraint accedes to the owner's desire for a living space that succumbs to the same enlightened anonymity he finds so refreshing on his stays in luxury hotels abroad. The apartment, in a postwar highrise, offered two amenities, light and views of Central Park, but was otherwise undistinguished. The architects tore out all internal walls, then screened areas with translucent panels which move, pivot or hinge in response to varying degrees of privacy. The apartment provides all the necessities of an impeccably-appointed hotel suite.

above *Although fabricated of modernist materials—sand-blasted glass framed by aluminum—the panels recall ageless shoji screens.*

opposite *A lacquered platform and dropped ceiling canopy draw the eye to the window wall and its park view.*

photography by *Paul Warchol*

Timeless design requires thinking in a new dimension that ignores conventional references.

left *The architects term the furnishings and accessories throughout the "suite" as "incidental," as they appear to float within the space. Ebonized oak floors and a banded sisal-like rug heighten the floating effect.*

above *A suspended, gridded system that accommodates the pivoting panels also screens track lighting. Ash wall in the hall conceals storage; wall opposite is painted. Chairs are by Mario Bellini; the table is Japanese.*

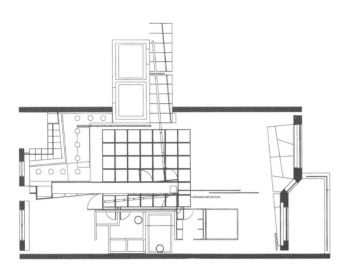

above *The architects clad the bath in one-foot-square tiles of green glass. The stainless steel sink, from Italy, stands against a wall of mirror. Cove lighting casts a warm glow over all.*

left *The kitchen and dining area directly adjoin the living area. Appliances are seamlessly integrated into an architectural unit composed of ash cabinetry, black granite countertops, and stainless steel backsplash. The corrugated wall conceals the service entrance and laundry.*

opposite *The unit that houses the bed incorporates storage as well. Silk draperies pull close for privacy and to cut light.*

ALBERTO GARDINO
Illuminating the Past

To many people—not only designers—an impression of timelessness resonates as much in recall as in fact, inciting a visceral response that feels at once subliminal and preordained. When architect Alberto Gardino was invited to reconceptualize the 1950s apartment that had been the boyhood home of a business administrator, he was given free rein to gut and reorganize its layout, but was asked to respect memories of the past by shedding new light—quite literally—on a collection of mementoes and souvenirs, such as a barber's chair and a ship's model that belonged to the owner's father. Gardino devised an essentially open plan, free of conventional doorways, that harnesses light from both ends of the apartment and allows freedom of movement throughout for the businessman, his wife, and their infant daughter. Marble, a material that has been ubiquitous in Italian construction for centuries, is presented in myriad guises, while furnishings are few and essential to comfort.

above *In the living room, two Eileen Gray sofas face each other across a floor of a red marble indigenous to Verona.*

opposite *A series of room-wide shelves consolidates the owners' books and collections. Windows are scrimmed in a translucent cotton/linen to diffuse light.*

photography by *Walter Prina*

left *Marble-and-etched-glass interior loggias access the entryway and kitchen on either side of the dining area. The barber's chair, a memento, visually converses with a contemporary armchair of Gardino's design.*

below *The dining area plays on the square and rectangle; even the ebony table base echoes the theme. Marble comes from Carrara, a quarry favored by Michelangelo.*

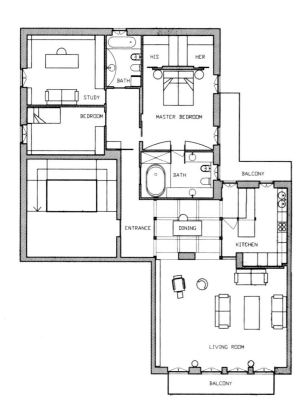

above *The master bedroom resorts to optical tactics to animate standard notions of intimacy and privacy: a marble alcove recesses the glass door to the bath so that it almost disappears; when opened, the bedroom door slides over its adjoining mirror—and thus transforms the room into a semi-public space.*

Timeless design defies fashion, and, instead, represents universal, intimate truths.

CLASSICAL

When designing a residence that will preserve an impression of time-lessness, traditional decorating precepts cannot be ignored. Harmonies of proportion, scale, texture, pattern, and color affect every aspect of a comfortable interior plan, from the selection and arrangement of the furnishings to traffic flow to lighting schemes which negotiate a balance between natural and artificial sources.

MARY DOUGLAS DRYSDALE
Capitalizing on Color

Nothing dates an interior like color. Designers intent upon achieving a timeless look often resort to a monochromatic palette. Mary Douglas Drysdale counters that notion even though she feels that interiors can only remain comfortable for the long term if they are not "style-centric." This philosophy is no more strikingly evident than in her own home, a four-story, Beaux Arts-style house erected in 1923. Rejuvenating the interiors has been an ongoing project for Drysdale since she and her husband purchased the house almost 15 years ago. The last significant phase was completed in 1994, but, as any designer will tell you, a happy house will always be the beneficiary of minor adjustments and exciting acquisitions. Drysdale replaced the entire infrastructure of the house, designed new woodwork to embellish every room, then granted each floor its own color scheme: the parlor floor, for instance, is a study in yellow and white while the first floor takes liberties with blacks and reds.

above *Drysdale designed the elegant, velvet-covered recamiers that flank the fireplace in the living room.*

photography by
Peter Vitale

above *The broad, stately proportions of the living room—18 feet by 32 feet by 11 feet high—are dramatized by the formal, yet companionable seating groups. Yellow proves an exhilarating foil to the interrelated ensembles.*

overleaf *The sitting room prevails upon architectural symmetries to lend an air of unwavering stability. Puddled draperies are subtly echoed in rug-tickling armchair and hassock covers. Rug is wool sisal.*

A timeless design respects the past, recognizes the present, and anticipates future needs.

above *An overscaled yellow plaid defines the living room draperies. Drysdale designed the sofa; the standing plaster statue is by Manuel Neri.*

left *The dining room features custom-painted chinoiserie motifs on the walls. The floor was left bare. Table and chairs don cheerful, fanciful covers when Drysdale and her husband entertain.*

left *The third floor, devoted to the master suite, assumes a soft, flattering apricot-and-cream palette. Drysdale even designed the secretary in an apricot hue.*

right *Drysdale's own dressing room/bath is centered with an ingenious, luxurious island fitted out with drawers of every depth and size. Walls on either side of the window display a collection of mirrors; the mirrored wall conceals closets.*

below *The wall paneling in the master bedroom, its bed, and side tables were planned, designed and painted as a suite.*

BUTTRICK, WHITE AND BURTIS
Crafted to Endure

In many cultures (including our own not so long ago), several generations of the same family expected to live under one roof; houses, therefore, were constructed to last. Today's families rarely share, except, perhaps, on holiday. This family compound on the Connecticut shore is one of that rare breed: it was designed to be enjoyed by several generations. Not only are its architects and clients one and the same, but they are related to each other by blood. The house they planned to cohabit had to function equally well when two people are in residence as when the entire tribe assembles. To avert internecine squabbles, the two couples—Harold Buttrick, FAIA and his son, designer Jerome Buttrick, and their wives—mutually arrived at the following job descriptions: architect, client, designer, critic. Their house takes its cue from a classic Yankee archetype: the shingled cottage, and its turn-of-the-century offspring, "The Shingled Cottage," notably McKim, Mead & White's Lowe broad-roofed bungalow in Rhode Island.

above *The Buttrick house refers to the Shingle Style. Stripped of unessential ornament, the house looks strikingly contemporary, yet rooted to its granite ridge, as if it had been there for ages.*

photography by
Eduard Hueber

Timeless houses are designed and constructed to weather the vagaries of taste.

above *The "great hall" steps up from the entry in a grand gesture of welcome. A subtly angled beam and white-oak plank flooring sweep through the space. The chest is a German copy of an 18th-century French piece.*

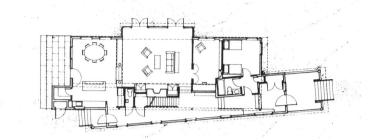

left *A muntined window wall, penetrated by a set of French doors and capped with transoms, separates the living room from the library and draws light through and across the contiguous spaces.*

above *Living room furnishings, kept to a spartan minimum, draw close to the hearth. The chimney wall, concealing cupboards and stereo speakers, is accented with grids. Coffee table base: Noguchi.*

opposite *Interior levels follow the ridge on which the house rests; thus the dining room and kitchen lie three steps lower than the living room and library. Windows, and doors leading out onto the ridge, are all crafted of solid mahogany.*

above *Storage in the kitchen, and throughout the house, is positioned for ease of access and designed to be discreet and blend in with the architecture. The backsplash, like the chimney wall, has a faintly Arts & Crafts feeling. Countertops are also mahogany.*

TRANSIT DESIGN
Upholding a Tradition

Italy sustains a strong tradition of loyalty to family. Sons and daughters follow their parents into commerce, live close to each other, and dine together on Sundays. A late-19th-century apartment building situated near a square designed by Piranesi in Rome testifies to this convention. Owned by a professional couple—he is in the Italian Senate and she is a practicing psychoanalyst—the building was subdivided into four apartments; the one featured here belongs to the parents, the others, to their three grown children. The reconfiguration of the building mandated extensive reconstruction. When the couple approached Transit Design—Giovanni Ascarelli, Maurizio Macciocchi, Danilo Parisio—they asked that architectural elements introduced into the apartment "look as if they had been there forever." And they do.

above *The* salotto, *or living room, located on the upper level of the apartment, is dominated by a seventeenth-century chinoiserie secretary that was made in Genoa.*

opposite *In deference to the architecture and scale of the room, upholstered furniture wears plain white linen; framed cotton batiste scrims are pulled taut over the arched windows. Painting is by Mario Schifano.*

photography by
Pietro Mari

above *The architectural plan is conducive to private reflection as well as to entertaining. The secretary is inlaid with mirrors to reflect light and amplify space.*

left *The landing adjacent to the salotto on the upper floor is where the entire family reunites to dine. White cotton slipcovers "dissolve" armless chairs of allusions to age or provenance.*

right *The dining table on the landing extends to seat twelve. Armchairs, like the table, date to the eighteenth century, and were modeled to appeal to a British market.*

right *The late-19th-century leather couch in the office, imported from Freudian-era Austria, assumes the familiar reclining shape used in therapy.*

left *The bookcase wall in the psychoanalyst's office is rendered in cherrywood; the double door at its center leads to a private bath and small closet.*

below *With its built-in daybed, the senator's office, adjacent to his wife's, also functions as guest room. The ceiling, original to the building, was painted white to conform to the rest of the apartment.*

ORLANDO DIAZ-AZCUY
Eternally Eclectic

Asserting a sense of timelessness within an existing architectural framework enjoins the designer to come to terms with issues of ego, period and restraint. Some ignore the context and rebuild from scratch; others, like San Francisco designer Orlando Diaz-Azcuy, invite the architecture to participate in an ongoing dialogue. The apartment featured here is in a building erected a few years after the 1906 Fire in a French Beaux-Arts style that felt reassuringly stable and enduring. The designer wanted to respect the period without recreating the past; this building, after all, was not indigenous to this place. So well-designed and constructed was the apartment, that the floor plan needed no reconfiguring. Well-known for his contemporary work, Diaz-Azcuy allowed himself to streamline in prudent ways: A monochromatic palette prevails, and furnishings are choice and few, in an eclectic blend. Eclecticism most truthfully expresses timelessness, he says, as it surrenders to no particular style.

above *The hallway sets the tone for the entire apartment. Subtle marbleizing accents door frames and cornices.*

right *Diaz-Azcuy ebonized the floors throughout; a pair of wool sisal rugs softens the effect in the living and dining rooms, which are contiguous to each other.*

photography by
J. D. Peterson

left *Diaz-Azcuy grouped the furniture at or near its perimeter, and left the center of the room free, to visually expand the limits of the living room; this strategy also facilitates passage to the dining room where a Gothic Revival chandelier, French grisaille panel and table in the Neoclassical mode commingle.*

opposite To capitalize on views of Alcatraz and San Francisco Bay, floor-to-ceiling French doors in the living and dining rooms are adorned only with white balloon shades. Gilt chair, circa 1850, is Neopolitan; the Adam-style painted commode is English.

left The cozy library was deliberately designed to contrast in mood and hue with the rest of the apartment. The ceiling is gilded; the twin recamiers are covered, legs and all, in velvet.

POWELL/KLEINSCHMIDT
Lofty Aspirations

History sweeps many architectural styles into its embrace; some endure, some thankfully fade away. In many cities, Chicago among them, the skyline has been defined by one paramount building type: the skyscraper. Early modernist prototypes, designed by premier architects of their day, continue to hold their own and are the standard against which many later examples are set. A 1957 lift-slab apartment building by Milton Schwartz is a case in point. A pair of graphic designers purchased three apartments on one of the building's higher floors, then retained Donald Powell and Robert Kleinschmidt and their firm to create a loft from the combined spaces. Powell/Kleinschmidt respected the integrity of the curtain wall—the floor-to-ceiling swath of glass looks out to an extraordinary 360-degree view—so they concentrated all services at the core, thereby freeing up the entire perimeter of the loft for living, entertaining, and sleeping, as well as for a collection of furniture from the 1950s and '60s—and a newborn baby.

above *The entry wall is fitted out with a bookcase. Floors throughout the loft are rendered in ash. Recessed lighting relieves the walls of obtrusive fixtures. Wall at right curls into the loft.*

photography by
Don DuBroff

left *The sponge-painted, plastered parabolic wall guides the eye around the kitchen/service core into the public spaces—and on to the views. Sculpture is by Lincoln Schatz.*

below *The living area is divided into two zones by a low cabinet housing the stereo. A pair of Breuer chairs, which predate the building by only two years, keeps company with a cabinet by Charles Eames. Most windows are left bare; a yellow drapery creates a pool of privacy in one corner.*

previous The galley kitchen opens to the dining area via a narrow pass-through supplemented by a blue counter used for breakfasts, or a bar. A "bubble lamp" by George Nelson hangs over the dining table. Chairs are by Charles Eames and Harry Bertoia.

below The master bedroom and its adjoining bath are linked by a carpet that was set into the floor. The interior corridor leads past the bath and closets to the kitchen core. The closets back onto a second bedroom.

right It was only when furnishings were in place that the owners decided to paint the bookcase wall in their master bedroom a strong shade of delphinium. The curtain, installed on a narrow steel rod several inches in from the curtain wall, is made of black, light-absorbent silk.

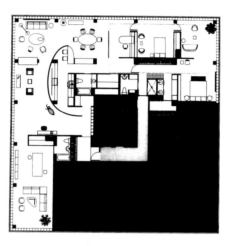

PERRY, DEAN, ROGERS & PARTNERS
Plainspoken Palladian

It is a well-known axiom that history repeats itself. Architecture too. To create an atmosphere of time-lessness, architects often straddle the centuries, borrowing literally and/or conceptually from buildings they admire from other periods and places. For Frank McGuire, AIA, a principal with the firm Perry, Dean, Rogers & Partners, the summer house he designed with and for his wife (and young daughter) near the Massachusetts/Rhode Island border culls, collects and contains cherished memories and "deepest feelings" of her girlhood vacations in this part of the world and a sojourn they shared in Italy. Although diminutive in size, their Villa Amanda creates an impression of comfortable grandeur overlaid with New England charm. Like a Palladian villa, the house is an exercise in symmetries, with duplicated front and rear elevations high-lighted by matching exterior stairways, and mirror-image interior spaces. Like its colonial forebears, its center-chimney floor plan is resolutely plain, with an updated keeping room, two bedrooms and studio aerie.

above *Board-skirted piers elevate the shingled villa above the flood plain, and allow the house expansive views to the nearby river.*

photography by
Steve Rosenthal

above *The house is furnished in a forthright manner, relying only on the basics. Floorboards are painted in a checkerboard pattern common to many "American Country" dwellingplaces.*

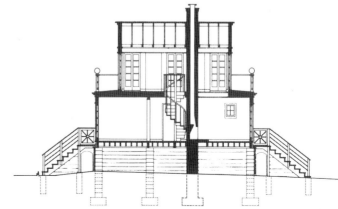

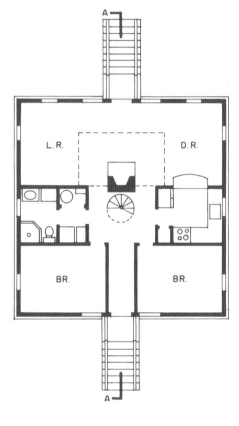

above *The living room end of the keeping room, or "gallery," eluci-dates what the architect calls "an economy of means." Accessories are few; instead a play of shadow, light and pattern animates the pale-hued spartan space.*

above *The upstairs studio, ringed by decks, overlooks the chimneypiece and stair. These, brightly enameled in canary and vermilion, provide the only jolts of hot color in the house.*

SHELTON, MINDEL & ASSOCIATES
A Cozy Compound

If one equated design with etiquette, timeless structures would be remarked upon for their sense of chivalry. Even if they stand out from their surroundings, they appear to respect and honor them as well; they make every effort to be good neighbors. The utterly prosaic asbestos cottage architect Lee Mindel purchased in the upscale Hamptons would have benefited from even the most minimal of improvements, but Mindel, courteous to a fault, decided to create a weekend getaway that would seamlessly integrate structure, site, and garden so that it would look as if the renovated cottage (and outbuildings) had been part of its Southampton, New York, neighborhood for years. He kept the roof height consistent with other houses in the area, clad both old and new structures with shingles, and constructed a series of garden spaces to function as "outdoor rooms." Picket fencing, a trellised pergola, a small pool and patio complete the compound.

above *Instead of razing the old asbestos eyesore and erecting a larger house, Lee Mindel opted for a series of small, cozy buildings, each of which is totally private unto itself.*

photography by
Dan Cornish

above *The separate structures in the Mindel compound share an intimacy of scale; rooflines echo each other, as does fenestration. Shingles will weather to a soft grey.*

left *The ceiling in the guest house/garage rises to 20 feet to accommodate a sleeping loft over the portion of the space allotted to the car. The dado in the guest quarters was made of standard 4-foot by 8-foot plywood sheets; varnished strips mask seams.*

opposite *The guest cottage is just steps away from the main house, visible through the over-sized window. Framed tax maps of Southampton ring the space above the dado.*

above *The view from the dining room looks past the living room and porch to the garden "rooms." Walls were painted a pale buttercream, a color Mindel calls "diffused light." The fanciful clock on the stair is by André Debreuil.*

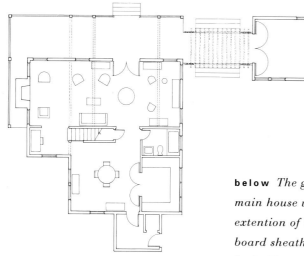

below *The ground floor of the main house was conceived as an extention of the porch; beaded board sheathes the ceilings of both. Floors are whitewashed Douglas fir. The chandelier over the dining table sports a flirty tutu, to hide lightbulbs.*

above *The dormer window in one of the upstairs bedrooms in the main cottage aligns with a matching window that was cut into the porch roof to extend the view out to the garden.*

opposite *The ceiling in the master bedroom looks as artfully folded as origami. The fruitwood column is Swedish. The bust is formed of codestone, named for its inventor, Eleanor Code, who invented the faux-marble mix so outdoor sculptures could withstand the elements.*

BYRNS, KENDALL & SCHIEFERDECKER
A Natural Perspective

Even if a design is tethered to the moment of its creation, it is often best appreciated from the perspective of some years—if not decades, or longer. The most resilient designs emerge and stand out from a continuum. For a residence on the shores of Lake Michigan, Stephen F. Byrns, of Byrns, Kendall & Schieferdecker, Architects, drew his inspiration from that transitional period when several parallel movements—the Prairie School, American and English Arts & Crafts, and Viennese Secessionist among them—contemporaneously altered longstanding attitudes towards architecture and design. Byrns wanted to celebrate elements of these styles while addressing current issues of land and energy conservation. To integrate house and site, he worked with all-natural materials—wood, shakes, pebbles, marble, and stone. In essence, the house forms a companionable T punctuated with a striking tower; it is scaled and detailed to enrich its owners' casual lifestyle on the lake.

above *The exterior of the house hearkens to stick-built, Shingle Style antecedents. Ribbon windows flank the dramatic entry tower.*

photography by *James Yochum*

above In the living room, broad expanses of glass take in views to windswept dunes braceleting the lake. The fireplace is composed of New York bluestone. The ribbon-window motif is repeated here as transom windows and gridded white oak woodwork.

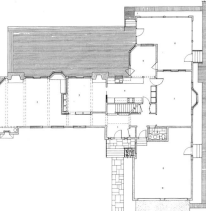

An enduring design both respects and stands out from its historical context.

above *Every plane in the interior hall and tower is sheathed in wood, a practice that recalls an age-old preference for keeping walls in summer houses plain and unadorned.*

left *The kitchen feels almost Zen-like in its simplicity. The paneling replicates the straightforward approach to wood taken by Craftsman Gustav Stickley.*

opposite *Individual balusters of the stairwell banister and upstairs railing are as elegantly and finely tuned as harpstrings.*

L. BOGDANOW & PARTNERS
Haven in the Woods

Americans have long entertertained a love affair with the outdoors, but, like Thoreau, often prefer to counterbalance the untamed with a civilizing shelter. Comfort, of course, means different things to different people. A tiny, nondescript 1970s builder's house that occupied a clearing in the woods overlooking a pond in Columbia County, New York, for instance, held no charm at all; indeed, it turned its back on the pond as if it were irrelevant. The site, though, was what attracted its new owner and his architect, Larry Bogdanow. To hold costs, Bogdanow retained the original footprint, but rotated the axis of the structure so that the house would focus on the view. Neither aggressive nor retiring, the renovated cabin is ingeniously assimilated into the rugged terrain by this maneuver, but also through a skillful use of materials, and especially a range of warm-toned woods such as cedar, maple, cherry and Douglas fir. Interiors were kept as simple as possible. Thoreau would have approved.

above *The cabin's broad-pitched roof and sheltering porch hearken to bungalows of the 1920s and '30s.*

opposite *The chimneypiece with inset shelves that encompasses the new fireplace was fabricated from shop-grade veneer-core cherry plywood.*

photography by
Ross Muir

Columbia County, New York   1,300 Square Feet • 121 Square Meters

opposite *With the addition of a second story, to accommodate a master suite and a deck, the square footage of the cabin was virtually doubled. The sense of spaciousness in the bedroom is reinforced by exploding the ceiling to the roofline and by painting the room, except beams and doors to the deck, all white.*

above *Cabinetry and open shelving in the kitchen is meticulously crafted, from cherrywood, with a Shaker-like precision. The layout sensibly concentrates the work area within an efficient U. Counter-tops are plastic laminate.*

right *The living room, which traverses the side of the house facing the pond, opens onto a screened porch. The interior focus of the room is the simple, sculptural fireplace. The room's economy of design is reflected in the plain-spoken arrangement of modernist furnishings.*

GORALNICK ★ BUCHANAN
A Serene Stateliness

In a way, designing a room or building that aspires to immortality is like a circus act; the architect has to be an expert juggler as well as a master illusionist. The Gilded Age witnessed the erection of a plethora of enormous houses for the New Rich which brazenly attempted to "juggle" and blend elements from myriad Old World sources. One of these, an enormous "summer cottage" in Lenox, Massachusetts, a fashionable watering hole of the period, had since gone through one unfortunate metamorphosis after another; in its last guise, it had been the headquarters of a religious cult. For a fund-raising decorators' showcase, Barry Goralnick and Michael Buchanan wanted to erase every vestige of the cult in the living room, return it to its original stateliness, and create a comfortable gathering place where people would feel at home, despite the room's size. Pools of bright, white seating affect the transition from intimidating to inviting, in a gesture of welcome that is, indeed, timeless.

above *At 46 feet in length, the living room could overwhelm, so the designers decided to divide it, with rugs, into cozier areas.*

opposite *Furnishings were purposely chosen from a variety of periods and styles; their eclecticism is united by the use of monochromatic white fabrics.*

photography by *Dan Cornish*

left *Existing architectural embellishments were faithfully restored; then the ceiling was painted deep blue to bring it down to human scale. Striped paper set in wall panels repeats the blue-and-white theme.*

above *A quiet corner of the living room was set apart for intimate dining or cards. Window coverings are a lightweight cotton-linen.*

MARK ZEFF
A Sophisticated Retreat

A vacation retreat often stands the test of time with greater aplomb than a permanent residence. This may come to pass in part because such getaways, by definition, are not occupied all year-round and, therefore, submit to all-too-understandable wear and tear only on an occasional basis. Perhaps, though, a vacation house can happen to appear ageless because the very concept of "being on holiday" indulges a less inhibited attitude towards its design and decoration. The result: A house that wears well because it is, in fact, easier to live in. New York designer Mark Zeff was called in a decade ago to decorate a beach house nestled amongst the sand dunes on a small peninsula licked both by freshwater and the ocean. His client wanted to retain the sense of elegance she was accustomed to in her winter home, but temper it with a practical approach to the salt-air environs. Zeff complied with a sand-inspired palette, and with room schemes that required little accessorizing.

above *The sitting room plays on pairs—of sofas, ebonywood planters' chairs, and coffee tables. Zeff designed the bases for the latter to support two Moroccan screens which he covered with glass.*

opposite *A family room directly adjoins the sitting room. Here a darker palette, in muted grass and sea tones prevails. Rugs in both rooms are 100 percent wool sisal.*

photography by *Eric Striffler and Mario Ruiz*

opposite *The angled walls in the dining room take in views of the water. Draperies are durable cotton duck. The chandelier and the base of the dining table were both designed with matching silhouettes by Zeff from hot rolled steel. Dining chairs are in the Chinese style.*

above *A simple chimneypiece and cherrywood mantel punctuate the flow of windows in the master bedroom. Duvet cover is an easy-care rayon/polyester blend.*

TRANSIT DESIGN
An Ageless Appeal

In Rome, many epochs collide—and collude—to create an urban environment that is, quite literally, "ageless." Individual neighborhoods, though, retain their own character and atmosphere. One of the most beautiful, and desirable, of these is Parioli, a genteel district that abuts the Borghese Gardens; over the years many embassies have moved here. The neighborhood held particular appeal, too, for a couple who collect Venetian paintings and contemporary glass from Murano. They wanted to showcase their pieces, and also to entertain friends on a regular basis. However, the apartment in a 1920s building they were attracted to required rehabilitation. The architects of Transit Design came to their rescue. Gutting the interiors, the firm reconfigured walls and openings to create vistas to the art and niches and cubbies to hold specific pieces of glass. At once introspective and inviting, the apartment now perfectly suits the art and satisfies its owners.

above *When Transit Design carved out the new spaces in the apartment, they reintroduced traditional doorways only where privacy was mandated.*

opposite *Although the palette is essentially neutral, bold splashes of color are tolerated as dramatic accents.*

photography by *Isidoro Genovese*

below *The terrace is partially sheltered by special scrims which lock into the gridded "trellis"; vines slowly being trained over the gridwork will eventually add further shade.*

above *Strict geometries—horizontal shelving displaying watercolors and prints, vertical latticework screening radiators, and a combination niche-cum-cupboard wall—set up energetic juxtapositions against the bare herringbone flooring.*

opposite *A set of Biedermeier chairs surrounds a dining room table designed by Transit's Danilo Parisio and fabricated from oxidized iron; the table comes apart in two longitudinal sections. The textured triptych over the Empire sideboard is by Burri.*

MARY DOUGLAS DRYSDALE
Framing a Collection

Collections of fine art, antiquities or treasured artifacts require a backdrop that will neither overwhelm the individual works nor intimidate their owners. Designer Mary Douglas Drysdale perfectly understood the parameters of her responsibility to an extensive collection of contemporary art glass when she was asked to orchestrate the interiors of a spacious town house in Washington, D.C. The owners wanted to rotate pieces from their 150-piece collection at whim, and feel confident that each time they brought out a new work, it could stand alone or within a group without upsetting the overall interior design. Drysdale made a strong yet circumspect architectural statement: gridded wall panels unite the public spaces. A creamy palette—not gallery white; not old-hat beige—enwraps clean-lined furnishings, books, and the glass in a way that the designer herself describes as unfussy, sophisticated, yet cozy. The fluency and translucence of glass is celebrated at every turn.

above *Drysdale designed an octagonal table and a console (in far window) to blend serenely with the architecture.*

opposite *The town house's atrium, girdled with railings made of gilded pipe metal, recalls the promenade decks of an ocean liner. Mirrored niches reflect artifacts. Oak flip-back chair is an early-20th-century antique.*

photography by *Andrew D. Lautman*

left *In the master bedroom, recessed shelves showcase blue glass. To accentuate the ceiling height, Drysdale dropped felt-trimmed curtains from custom poles attached where a cornice might run. Antique bronzed tacks stud the chimneypiece.*

below *A lushly-carpeted stair swings up from the vestibule to the atrium. The newel post acts as a pedestal for a bronze torso; at the top of the stair stands Elena Korakianitou's* Birth of Eros.

Pared down rooms and simple furnishings set off art of any period to its best advantage.

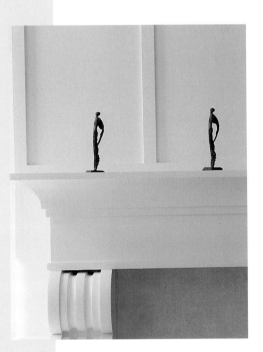

above *Arms and wings of a series of bronze angels by Avis Turner subtly echo the curve of the mantelpiece's cove molding.*

left *In the living room, gridded paneling frames and sets off individual pieces of sculpture and glass. As translucent Roman shades fall, pleats align with the grids. Twin chaises flank the fireplace. Maple zig-zag chairs were inspired by a Rietveld prototype of 1934. The ceramic horse sculpture is a Balossi.*

above *The designer took liberties with the mood of the kitchen by having artist Rebecca Cross paint whimsical peppers, kumquats and watermelon seeds over an arch and in the breakfast nook. Chairs are by Mario Villa.*

167

JANET SCHIRN
An Eclectic Elegance

Many interpreters of "timeless design" find they have to wrestle illogically conceived spaces into a suitable habitat for precious and lovely things; others must strike a balance between a perfectly acceptable environment and a medley of furnishings. Presented with a luxurious duplex in a vintage cooperative building on Chicago's Lake Shore Drive, designer Janet Schirn was gratified that an architectural overhaul of the living/dining sector of the apartment was unnecessary. The rooms were well proportioned and discreetly embellished; all she had to add was a fireplace. Schirn's main mission, therefore, was to merge the owners' tastes—his modern, hers 18th century. Tactfully averting potential stylistic discord, the designer dissolved the room schemes of color. Upholstery and window treatments are white, the background, a muted celadon, a cool neutral which recently entered interior design's pantheon of timeless hues.

above *Designer Schirn experimented with a number of furniture arrangements before her clients agreed upon two seating groups which flank the new fireplace. Nude over sofa is by Michael Cheny.*

photography by
Mary Nichols

above *Window treatments consist of swags tossed, like scarves, over tension bars, which free views to the lake.*

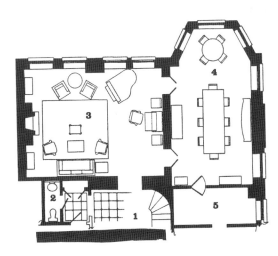

opposite *To underscore and reinforce the cohesion and compatibility of the living and dining rooms, designer Schirn repeated her swagged window treatment.*

above *The dining room is spacious enough to accommodate a traditional grouping used for formal entertaining plus a casual table in the window.*

DIRECTORY

Architects & Interior Designers

Buttrick, White & Burtis
Harold Buttrick
Jerome Buttrick
475 Tenth Avenue
New York, New York 10013
United States
Tel: (212) 967-3333
Fax: (212) 629-3749

Byrns, Kendall & Schieferdecker
Architects
Stephen F. Byrns
11 West 25th Street
New York, New York 10010
United States
Tel: (212) 807-0127
Fax: (212) 727-9067

Dennis Jenkins Associates
Dennis Jenkins
5813 Southwest 68th Street
South Miami, Florida 33143
United States
Tel: (305) 665-6960
Fax: (305) 665-6971

Di Cicco Vinci • Ahn Architects
Carol Di Cicco Vinci
James Ahn
135 Fifth Avenue
New York, New York 10010
United States
Tel: (212) 673-5495

Drysdale Design Associates
Mary Douglas Drysdale
1733 Connecticut Avenue, N.W.
Washington, D.C. 20008
United States
Tel: (202) 588-0700
Fax: (202) 588-5086

ELS/Elbasani & Logan Architects
Donn Logan
Marcy Li Wong
2040 Addison Street
Berkeley, California 94704
United States
Tel: (510) 549-2929
Fax: (510) 843-3304

Ford, Powell & Carson, Inc.
Chris Carson
John Gutzler
1138 East Commerce Street
San Antonio, Texas 78205
United States
Tel: (210) 226-1246
Fax: (210) 226-6482

Fortune Design
Cay Fortune
5505 Lake Washington Boulevard, NE
Suite #1D
Kirkland, Washington 98033
United States
Tel: (206) 889-9377
Fax: (206) 889-9777

Goodman Charlton, Inc.
Jeffrey Goodman
Steven Charlton
1500 Rising Glen Road
Los Angeles, California 90069
United States
Tel: (310) 657-7068
Fax: (310) 657-1868

Goralnick ★ Buchanan Design
Barry Goralnick
Michael Buchanan
306 East 61st Street
New York, New York 10021
United States
Tel: (212) 644-0334
Fax: (212) 644-0904

Hugh Newell Jacobsen
2529 P Street, N.W.
Washington, D.C. 20007
United States
Tel: (202) 337-5200
Fax: (202) 337-3609

Janet Schirn Design Group
Janet Schirn
401 North Franklin
Chicago, Illinois 60610
United States
Tel: (312) 222-0017
Fax: (312) 222-1465

L. Bogdanow & Partners Architects
Larry Bogdanow
75 Spring Street
New York, New York 10012
United States
Tel: (212) 966-0313
Fax: (212) 941-8875

Legorreta Arquitectos
Victor Legorreta
Palacio de Versalles 285A
Mexico City 11020
Mexico
Tel: 011-525-2519698
Fax: 011-525-5966162

Emanuela Frattini Magnusson
588 Broadway
Suite 809
New York, New York 10012
United States
Tel: (212) 925-4500
Fax: (212) 925-4525

Mark Zeff Consulting
Mark Zeff
260 West 72nd Street
Suite 12B
New York, New York 10023
United States
Tel: (212) 580-7090
Fax: (212) 580-7181

Arthur de Mattos Casas
Al. Ministro Rocha Azevedo 1052
São Paulo, São Paulo 01410002
Brazil
Tel: 011-55-11-2826311
Fax: 011-55-11-2826608

Nagle Hartray & Associates, Ltd.
James L. Nagle
One IBM Plaza
Chicago, Illinois 60611
United States
Tel: (312) 832-6900
Fax: (312) 832-0004

Olson Sundberg Architects, Inc.
Jim Olson
108 First Avenue South
Fourth Floor
Seattle, Washington 98104
United States
Tel: (206) 624-5670
Fax: (206) 624-3730

Orlando Diaz-Azcuy Designs
Orlando Diaz-Azcuy
45 Maiden Lane
San Francisco, California 94108
United States
Tel: (415) 362-4500
Fax: (415) 788-2311

Parsons + Fernandez-Casteleiro, P.C.
Jeff Parsons
Manuel Fernandez-Casteleiro
62 White Street
New York, New York 10013
United States
Tel: (212) 431-4310
Fax: (212) 431-4310

Perry, Dean, Rogers & Partners
Frank McGuire
177 Milk Street
Boston, Massachusetts 02109
United States
Tel: (617) 423-0100
Fax: (617) 426-2274

Powell/Kleinschmidt
Donald Powell
Robert Kleinschmidt
645 North Michigan Avenue
Suite 810
Chicago, Illinois 60611
United States
Tel: (312) 642-6450
Fax: (312) 642-5135

Shelton, Mindel & Associates
Lee Mindel
216 West 18th Street
New York, New York 10011
United States
Tel: (212) 243-3939
Fax: (212) 727-7310

Studio Gardino Architettura
Alberto Gardino
Via Annunciata 23-2
20121 Milan
Italy
Tel: 011-39-2-6551955
Fax: 011-39-2-6551955

Angelo Tartaglia
Via Boezio 92, D 9A
00192 Rome
Italy
Tel: 011-39-6-6873879
Fax: 011-39-6-6868449

Thad Hayes Design
Thad Hayes
90 West Broadway #2A
New York, New York 10007
United States
Tel: (212) 571-1234
Fax: (212) 571-1239

Transit Design Srl
Giovanni Ascarelli
Maurizio Macciocchi
Danilo Parisio
Via Emilio Morosini, 17
00153 Rome
Italy
Tel: 011-39-6-5899848
Fax: 011-39-6-5899893

Zyscovich Architects
Bernard Zyscovich
New World Tower
100 North Biscayne Boulevard
Miami, Florida 33132
United States
Tel: (305) 372-5222

Photographers

Edoardo d'Antona
Via Montesanto 12
00195 Rome
Italy
Tel: 011-39-6-5600226

Jaime Ardiles-Arce
730 Fifth Avenue
New York, New York 10019
United States
Tel: (212) 333-8779
Fax: (212) 593-2070

Dan Cornish
38 Evergreen Road
New Canaan, Connecticut 06840
United States
Tel: (203) 972-3714
Fax: (203) 972-1910

Don DuBroff
101 South Catherine Avenue
La Grange, Illinois 60525
United States
Tel: (708) 482-0945
Fax: (708) 482-0965

Jürgen Frank
350 West 51st Street #17B
New York, New York 10019
United States
Tel: (212) 581-6501
Fax: (212) 541-5802

Isidoro Genovese
Via E. Faa. di Bruno 87
00195 Rome
Italy
Tel: 011-39-6-37513679

Hedrich Blessing
Jim Hedrich
11 West Illinois Street
Chicago, Illinois 60610
United States
Tel: (312) 321-1151

Hickey-Robertson
Blaine Hickey
Ogden Robertson
1318 Sul Ross
Houston, Texas 77006
United States
Tel: (713) 522-7258

Eduard Hueber
51 White Street
New York, New York 10013
United States
Tel: (212) 941-9294
Fax: (212) 941-9317

Michael Jensen
655 Northwest 76th Street
Seattle, Washington 98117
United States
Tel: (206) 789-7693

Lautman Photography
Andrew D. Lautman
Robert C. Lautman
4906 41st Street, N.W.
Washington, D.C. 20016
United States
Tel: (202) 966-2800
Fax: (202) 966-4240

Lourdes Legorreta
Sierra Nevada 460
Mexico City 11000
Mexico
Tel: 011-525-5200745
Fax: 011-525-5204045

Pietro Mari
Rome
Italy
Tel: 011-39-6-4741241

Michael Moran Photography
Michael Moran
245 Mulberry Street #14
New York, New York 10012
United States
Tel: (212) 226-2596
Fax: (212) 219-1566

Michael Mundy
25 Mercer Street
New York, New York 10013
United States
Tel: (212) 226-4741
Fax: (212) 343-2936

Mary E. Nichols
250 South Larchmont Boulevard
Los Angeles, California 90004
United States
Tel: (213) 935-3080

Paul Warchol Photography
Paul Warchol
133 Mulberry Street
New York, New York 10013
United States
Tel: (212) 431-3461
Fax: (212) 274-1953

Peter Vitale Photography
Peter Vitale
P.O. Box 10126
Santa Fe, New Mexico 87504
United States
Tel: (505) 988-2558

J. D. Peterson
530 Hampshire #303
San Francisco, California 94110
United States
Tel: (415) 861-3686

Walter Prina
Via Venini 30
20100 Milan
Italy
Tel: 011-39-2-2841369

Reinés Studio
Tuca Reinés
Rua Emanuel Kant 58
São Paulo, São Paulo 04536050
Brazil
Tel: 011-55-11-30619127
Fax: 011-55-11-8528735

Steve Rosenthal
59 Maple Street
Auburndale, Massachusetts 02186
United States
Tel: (617) 244-2986

Ross Muir Photography
Ross Muir
113 East 31st Street
New York, New York 10016
United States
Tel: (212) 779-3395

Mario Ruiz
425 Riverside Drive
New York, New York 10025
United States
Tel: (212) 316-2333
Fax: (212) 316-2431

Eric Striffler
P.O. Box 215
Watermill, New York 11976
United States
Tel: (516) 726-7376
Fax: (516) 726-5972

David Wakely
544 Vermont
San Francisco, California 94107
United States
Tel: (415) 861-7503

Nancy Robinson Watson
609 Ocean Drive #7-H
Key Biscayne, Florida 33149
United States
Tel: (305) 361-9182
Fax: (305) 361-6791

James Yochum
P.O. Box 427
Sawyer, Michigan 49125
United States
Tel: (312) 829-5434

INDEX

Acknowledgments

Despite the single author's name on a cover and title page, a book is always a team effort. For the contributions and encouragement of the following participants, I am ever grateful:

to the architects and designers, who shared their work, and their vision of what they believe to be timeless

to the photographers, who so eloquently translate three into two dimensions

to the staff of PBC, who assiduously transport every image and every word through the editorial and production process

to the designer of the book, Garrett Schuh, who created pages that are, indeed, inherently timeless in their appeal

to Wendy Moonan, for her Foreword and friendship

to my family, for their patience and support

and, finally, to the Design Writers Group, who motivate and inspire me by their collective example, and especially to Dylan Landis who introduced me to PBC